Aberdeenshire Library and Information Service
www.aberdeenshire.gov.uk.libraries
Renewals Hotline 01224 661511

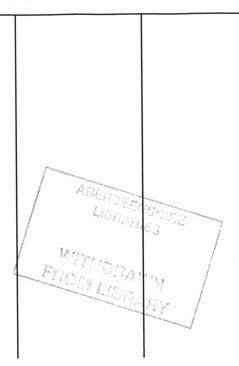

BAGE, Grant

Prison break!

Prison Break!

And Other Adventures Underground

Grant Bage and Jane Turner

A & C Black • London

Produced for A & C Black by
Monkey Puzzle Media Ltd
The Rectory, Eyke, Woodbridge
Suffolk IP12 2QW, UK

Published by A & C Black Publishers Limited
38 Soho Square, London W1D 3HB

First published 2008
Copyright © 2008 A & C Black Publishers Limited

ISBN 978-1-4081-0019-6 (hardback)
ISBN 978-1-4081-0118-6 (paperback)

A CIP catalogue record for this book is available from the British Library.

Editor: Cath Senker
Design: Mayer Media Ltd
Picture research: Lynda Lines
Series consultant: Jane Turner

This book is produced using paper that is made from wood grown in managed, sustainable forests. It is natural, renewable and recyclable. The logging and manufacturing processes conform to the environmental regulations of the country of origin.

Printed in China by C & C Offset Printing Co., Ltd

Picture acknowledgements
akg-images p. 9; Alamy pp. 11 (blickwinkel), 15 (qaphotos), 16 (Iain Masterton), 22 (Visual Arts Library); Corbis pp. 12 (Kim Ludbrook/epa), 18 (Bettmann), 25 (Yann Arthus-Bertrand), 27 (Bettmann), 29 left (Jonathan Blair); FLPA p. 6 (Phil McLean); Getty Images pp. 7, 10 (Stephen Alvarez), 14 (AFP), 17 (Boyer/Roger Viollet), 24 (Marvin E Newman), 26 (Hulton Archive); Kobal Collection pp. 4, 8 (Sat.1); Rex Features pp. 1 (Sipa), 13 (Sipa), 20 (Brando Quilici/Agentur Focus), 21 (Roger Viollet), 29 right (Denise Bradley/EDPPICS); Ronald Grant Archive p. 5 (United Artists); Topfoto p. 23; USGS p. 19. Artwork on pp. 28, 29 bottom by Michael Posen

The front cover shows a cell in the prison on Alcatraz Island, California, USA (Alamy/Mike Long).

Every effort has been made to contact copyright holders of material reproduced in this book. Any omissions will be rectified in subsequent printings if notice is given to the publishers.

CONTENTS

The great escape 4

The wooden horse 6

Tunnelling to freedom 8

How low can you go? 10

Digging for the devil 12

Getting wet to stay dry 14

Speed underground 16

Alive below 18

Mummy – help! 20

The biggest thing ever buried? 22

Bones, bodies and burials 24

Alive underground? 26

Little rock monsters 28

Glossary 30

Further information 31

Index 32

Abbreviations **m** stands for metres • **ft** stands for feet • **in** stands for inches • **km** stands for kilometres • **°C** stands for degrees Centigrade • **°F** stands for degrees Fahrenheit

The great escape

In World War II, the Nazis thought they had built an escape-proof prison. They were wrong!

Stalag Luft III was a prison camp built on loose, sandy soil. The huts were raised off the ground. There were look-out towers all along the barbed-wire fence. But in 1944, through back-breaking, dangerous work, 76 **prisoners of war** tunnelled their way to freedom.

Fat candles

The prisoners skimmed mutton fat from their soup and moulded it into candles. Later the escapees managed to rig up electric lights in the tunnel!

Prisoners make a dash for freedom in this poster for The Great Escape, *the adventure film about the Stalag Luft III breakout.*

prisoners of war   soldiers put in prison by an enemy during a war

Extra cables and bulbs were added to the prison lighting circuit, stealing electricity and providing light for the diggers.

A scene from The Great Escape film. The Stalag Luft III escape tunnel, nicknamed "Harry", was 90 m (295 ft) long but not high enough to stand up in. It started under a stove in the prisoners' hut and ended in woods outside the camp fence.

The prisoners used wood from their beds to prop up the tunnel.

The prisoners used empty milk tins to **excavate** the sand.

excavate   remove earth or soil by digging

The wooden horse

One group of prisoners of war in a Nazi prison camp took up gymnastics. They didn't break out in a sweat: they broke out of Stalag Luft III!

In 1943, three British prisoners escaped using a horse — but they didn't ride it. It was a vaulting horse. While others jumped over it, one man could hide inside and dig a tunnel.

A mole can dig a 30 m (100 ft) tunnel in 10 hours — with just its paws!

I'm free!

Three men took 114 days to dig the tunnel with metal bowls.

A shot from the film about the wooden-horse escape. The noise of the prisoners jumping masked the sound of digging.

The tunnel was 30 m (100 ft) long.

Digging was dangerous work. Tunnellers survived at least one cave-in.

Cast out

One of the wooden-horse gymnasts, Peter Butterworth, became an actor after the war. He didn't get a part in the film about the escape though. The **casting director** said he "didn't look convincingly heroic and athletic enough"!

casting director   person who decides which actors will be in a film

Tunnelling to freedom

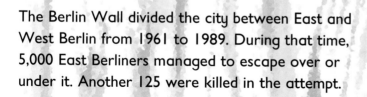

In the 1960s, East Berliners were imprisoned in their own city by a high, concrete wall. There were armed guards, barbed wire, guard dogs and landmines. Anyone trying to escape was shot.

The Berlin Wall divided the city between East and West Berlin from 1961 to 1989. During that time, 5,000 East Berliners managed to escape over or under it. Another 125 were killed in the attempt.

The soft soil under Berlin inspired some people to dig their way to freedom. There was one secret tunnel dug by students through a graveyard! People brought flowers to a grave. When nobody was looking, they dropped out of sight, down a long escape tunnel.

A scene from a film about a daring escape through a secret tunnel leading from East Berlin to the free West.

Dead give-away

The graveyard tunnel under the Berlin Wall was only discovered after a woman left her baby's pram at the surface.

landmine a bomb buried underground

Barbed wire

to prevent people from getting to the wall.

The concrete Berlin Wall was 3.75 m (12 ft) high and more than 150 km (93 miles) long.

Landmines under the ground would **blow up** anyone who walked over them.

Guards carried guns and would shoot anyone who tried to escape.

East German soldiers and barbed wire at the Berlin Wall.

9

How low can you go?

Some people explore tunnels for thrills. This is great fun – if you enjoy camping deep under the ground!

Cavers explore a world rarely visited by humans. They spend weeks in dark, cold caves, crawling along steep, narrow passages, and wading, swimming and diving through icy water.

In 2005, nine cavers broke the world depth record. They travelled more than 2,000 metres (6,600 feet) underground into the deepest known cave in the world, Krubera Cave in Russia. They pitched their tents and cooked meals 1,640 metres (5,400 feet) underground!

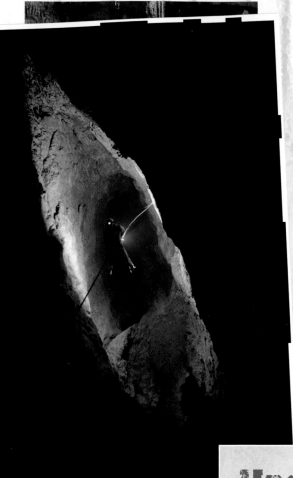

A caver entering Krubera Cave.

Underground science

Speleology is the scientific study of caves. Cavers (or spelunkers) investigate caves for fun!

impermeable does not let water through **permeable** lets water through

Stalactites are made from a chemical called **calcium carbonate**. They hang down from cave ceilings.

Clay is an **impermeable** rock: it does not let water through.

Caves are natural underground holes. This one is in Italy.

Caves are formed when **permeable limestone** rock is dissolved by rainwater or underground streams.

Stalagmites grow up from cave floors, often in strange shapes.

limestone rock formed from the skeletons and shells of sea creatures

Digging for the devil

For some people, digging tunnels is just a day job. Miners work underground chipping out coal, tin and other valuable minerals.

An injured miner is carried out of Elandsrand mine.

Gold is buried in the rock beneath Johannesburg in South Africa. The only way to reach it is by digging **shafts** and sending miners thousands of metres underground. It is hard, hot and dangerous work. Gold mines are often called "the devil's workplace".

In 2007, 3,200 gold miners were trapped for 2 days. They were more than 2 km (6,600 ft) underground in Elandsrand mine, Johannesburg. It was 40°C (104°F) – hotter than a sauna – and the air was running out. Rescue came just in time.

Old gold

Gold is so precious that it is rarely wasted. Most of the gold ever found is still around today. The gold in your earring could once have been part of a Viking crown!

mineral   a substance that occurs naturally in rocks such as coal, tin and gold

Miners use powerful drills to remove the rocks that contain gold.

Miners drilling for gold in a South African gold mine.

The miner wears a light on his helmet so that his hands are free for work.

Gloves protect the miner's hands from sharp materials.

The hard hat protects the miner from falling rock.

shaft vertical passage with a lift that goes to the bottom of a mine

Getting wet to stay dry

Tunnel travel

The Channel Tunnel is 50.45 kilometres (31.35 miles) long and up to 60 metres (200 feet) deep. Eurostar trains take 20 minutes to travel from England to France. Cars, coaches and lorries take 35 minutes on shuttle trains.

A Eurostar train travelling between England and France.

Until the 1990s, a trip from England to France meant choppy waves and seasickness. Not any more!

In 1857, French **engineer** Thomé de Gamond dived deep to collect rock samples from the seabed. He had no breathing equipment — apart from his lungs! Thomé found a thick layer of waterproof **chalk**: easy to dig, but strong enough to make a tunnel. In 1994, the Channel Tunnel was completed.

engineer   someone who uses technology, mathematics and science to solve practical problems

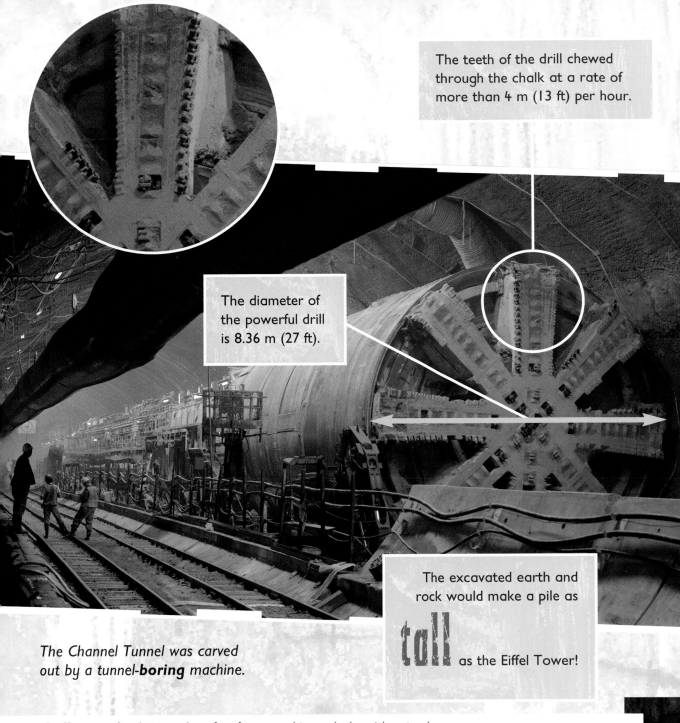

The teeth of the drill chewed through the chalk at a rate of more than 4 m (13 ft) per hour.

The diameter of the powerful drill is 8.36 m (27 ft).

The excavated earth and rock would make a pile as **tall** as the Eiffel Tower!

*The Channel Tunnel was carved out by a tunnel-**boring** machine.*

chalk a soft white rock   **boring** making a hole with a tool

Speed underground

Underground railways were invented in the 19th century. People wanted to escape the carriages, carts, horses and horse dung clogging the streets above.

What a stink!

In 2001, engineers put scent in London Underground's **ventilation** system. They had to stop doing it because the smell made people sick!

Nowadays, some modern cities could not work without underground railways. In Tokyo, Japan, 7.25 million people travel underground every day. There are guards whose job is to push and squeeze people into carriages!

The air underground is stale and hot. Every passenger heats the air, just by breathing. On average, the temperature underground is 10°C (18°F) higher than at the surface. It can get sweaty down there!

The first underground railways were built in New York, Paris and London. The easiest way was to dig a deep trench, lay a railway line along it, and then cover it back over with a road.

Tokyo travellers crammed into an underground train.

ventilation   bringing new air in and taking stale air out

The building of the underground railway in Paris, France, in 1901.

These buildings could 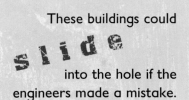 into the hole if the engineers made a mistake.

A crane like this can dig faster than 20 men.

This truck is being loaded with earth to be taken away.

A **w i d e** tunnel is dug for the narrow underground railway line.

Although it is an enormous tunnel, men with spades are still needed to finish it.

Alive below

Living underground sounds fun. But where would you hang your washing, fly your kite or walk your dog?

In August 1945 the world changed forever. The USA dropped **nuclear bombs** on Japan. The blast and nuclear poisons left in the air and water killed thousands.

In the 1950s, the governments in some countries were terrified of nuclear war. They built underground towns they could escape to in an emergency. One town in the UK even had its own railway station — so the queen could get there quickly if London was bombed!

The city of Hiroshima after it was hit by a nuclear bomb.

nuclear bomb   bomb that gets its explosive energy from splitting atoms

In the USA today, there is a secret underground complex at Mount Weather, Virginia. In the case of a national emergency, the president will hurry there by helicopter.

Mount Weather is an ordinary mountain in the USA — except that inside it hides an underground complex for national emergencies.

Underground, there are tunnels so high they could contain office buildings three storeys high!

The sewage tanks in the complex can handle 30,000 toilet flushes every day.

Mount Weather is **TOP SECRET**. Photographs can be taken only from a distance.

The main compound contains 2,000 beds — but only the president has his own bedroom.

The president's helicopter is kept here.

Mummy – help!

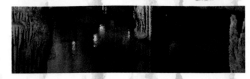

Discovering a secret tunnel, finding treasure and becoming famous sounds like a dream: but what if you end up cursed?

Howard Carter dug for 15 years in the Egyptian desert, searching for the tomb of the ancient king Tutankhamun. He had nearly run out of money when he found steps, hidden by sand. The steps led to a tunnel, to a tomb, to treasure and perhaps ... to a curse.

At last, Howard Carter and his helpers had found the tomb. Back in ancient times, spells had been cast to keep out intruders. Carter died 17 years AFTER finding Tutankhamun – so the spells did not work on him!

*This **mummy** was a living person 3,300 years ago. Tutankhamun was 9 years old when he became king and probably 18 when he died.*

Insides out

To preserve dead bodies, ancient Egyptians took out the insides that might rot. The brain was pulled out through the nose, using a special hook.

mummy   a body that has been treated to stop it from rotting, and then wrapped in cloth

The wind blows the sand, and it quickly covers buried objects.

Howard Carter's incredible find in 1923 — the tomb of Tutankhamun.

Rock walls kept Tutankhamun's body cool.

Any body home?

Howard Carter watches as Tutankhamun's funeral bed is removed.

These steps were covered in sand, so the tomb remained hidden for 3,000 years.

preserve   *stop something from rotting*

The biggest thing ever buried?

What is the last thing you might expect to find inside a hill? A *ship*!

For centuries, people in Sutton Hoo, in Suffolk, England had noticed 20 huge mounds of earth. What could they be? In the 1930s, archaeologists dug one up. They found hundreds of iron rivets in rows, but only traces of the planks the ship had been built from. Everything wooden had rotted in the sand. Then they discovered a helmet, sword, gold coins and other beautiful things.

The mound had been made to honour a Saxon king, about 1,400 years ago. His treasure was buried in one of his own ships to show the king's power, even after death.

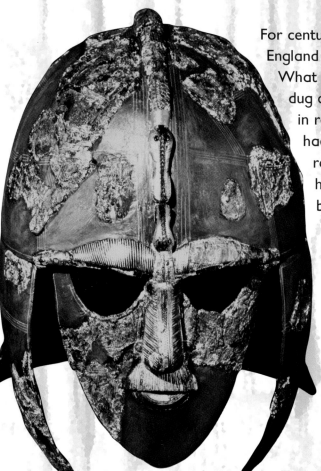

This stunning helmet was buried in the ship.

Dead wood

Dead wood doesn't simply rot away. It provides food. Bacteria and fungi can live on it. They munch it without mercy – the rotters!

bacteria   very tiny living things that are often a cause of disease

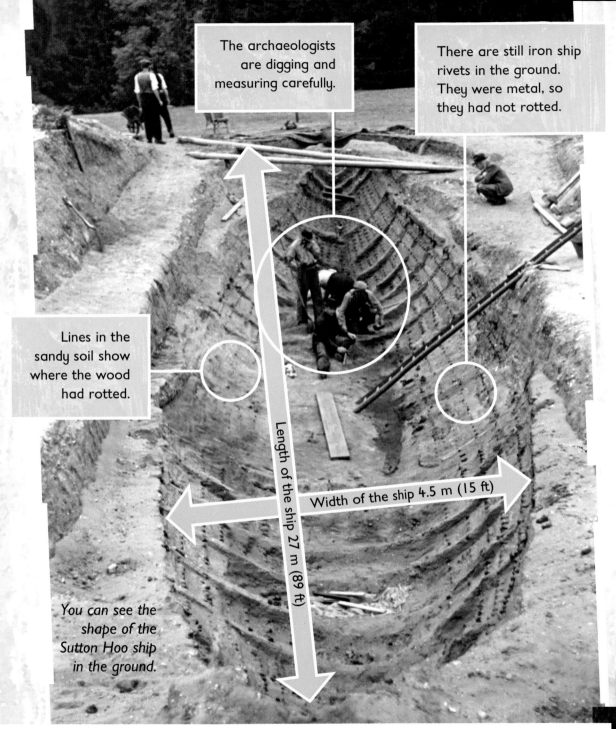

The archaeologists are digging and measuring carefully.

There are still iron ship rivets in the ground. They were metal, so they had not rotted.

Lines in the sandy soil show where the wood had rotted.

Length of the ship 27 m (89 ft)

Width of the ship 4.5 m (15 ft)

You can see the shape of the Sutton Hoo ship in the ground.

fungi group of living things including mushrooms and moulds

Bones, bodies and burials

Being dead and buried go together well – but what about storing dead bodies in TUNNELS?

In the past, people in some cities built tunnels called catacombs and placed dead bodies there. Today, the catacombs are filled with bones – or even whole bodies, if the tunnels are cold enough. Visit if you dare!

Morgues

A morgue is a cold room for keeping dead bodies, until it is known who they are and what they have died of. Morgues are even colder than catacombs. Bodies are kept frozen at between -15° and -25°C (5° to -13°F).

This Paris catacomb is for bones, not bodies. When graveyards became full, one solution was to pile up the bones underground.

In this catacomb, the body-rotting process slows down. A body may just dry out rather than rot away.

The flesh has rotted, leaving the skull.

The clothes remain.

Because of the cool temperature, the body has not completely rotted.

Living things start to rot a few minutes after dying. A catacomb is deep, dark and cool, and keeps bodies cold. It is like a fridge.

These bodies in a catacomb belonged to wealthy people in Sicily, Italy. They died between the 17th and 19th centuries.

Alive underground?

It would be your worst nightmare: to be sealed in a coffin when you are still alive.

Modern doctors use **sensors** to check when people are dead. Before these were invented, there were safety coffins with bells, whistles and flags to fly. They were vital if the doctor got it wrong and you woke up underground!

1 The man is buried in a coffin, as normal.

2 A special air shaft leads down to the coffin, so if he wakes up, he can breathe.

3 An electric wire is attached to the man's hands.

4 If he moves, the movement triggers an alarm bell and opens the lid of the air shaft.

This German safety coffin from 1878 made sure the person inside could escape if buried alive by mistake.

sensor detecting instrument

Harry Houdini was a famous magician. In 1926, he was sealed inside a coffin and submerged in a swimming pool for 90 minutes. He survived.

Living on thin air

Houdini's coffin had enough air for only 3 to 4 minutes. Nobody knows how he survived. Houdini claimed he just breathed very lightly.

Harry Houdini climbing into his coffin, ready to be submerged in the swimming pool.

Little rock monsters

So kids know nothing, and rocks are boring? Wrong! Kids can find rocks that change the world.

Fossil finder

Mary Anning lived 200 years ago and never went to school. With her brother, she hunted fossils. Their first big find was when Mary was 12 years old.

These children's discoveries released monsters, trapped in stone. They had once been living dinosaurs, millions of years ago. When they died, mud covered their bodies — and preserved them.

2 If the mud is thick, it presses heavily on the body.

1 When a body is covered in wet mud, it rots more slowly than in the open air.

This illustration shows what a live pterosaur might have looked like.

Owain Lewis with the pterosaur bones he found.

Six-year-old Owain Lewis found the fossil bones of a flying reptile called a pterosaur on the Isle of Wight. He said, "Dad and me were looking for fossils and we spotted this one at exactly the same time. I knew straight away that it was a bit of a dinosaur because their bones are black and shiny."

3 Over hundreds of years, this weight can turn bones to stone. This is a fossil.

4 Over millions of years, the surface of the Earth can be lifted or folded, and the soil worn away by wind, rain and ice. Fossils can come to the surface.

Glossary

bacteria very tiny living things that are often a cause of disease

boring making a hole with a tool

calcium carbonate a chemical found in limestone

casting director person who decides which actors will be in a film

chalk a soft white rock

engineer someone who uses technology, mathematics and science to solve practical problems

excavate remove earth or soil by digging

fungi group of living things including mushrooms and moulds

impermeable does not let water through

landmine a bomb buried underground

limestone rock formed from the skeletons and shells of sea creatures

mineral a substance that occurs naturally in rocks such as coal, tin and gold

mummy a body that has been treated to stop it from rotting, and then wrapped in cloth

nuclear bomb bomb that gets its explosive energy from splitting atoms

permeable lets water through

preserve stop something from rotting

prisoners of war soldiers put in prison by an enemy during a war

sensor detecting instrument

shaft vertical passage with a lift that goes to the bottom of a mine

ventilation bringing new air in and taking stale air out

Further information

Books

Caves, Graves and Catacombs: Secrets from Beneath the Earth by Natalie Jane Prior (Allen & Unwin, 2003)
True stories about caves, graves, grave robbers, ancient sewer systems, cave dwellers, and more.

Fossil *(Eyewitness Guide)* by Paul D Taylor (Dorling Kindersley, 2003)
Excellent introductory guide to fossils.

Inside the Tomb of Tutankhamun by Jacqueline Morley (Book House, 2005)
Information about ancient Egypt, Tutankhamun and the story of Carter's tomb excavation.

Official Channel Tunnel Factfile by Philip Clark (Boxtree Ltd, 1996)
Includes the people and machines behind the project, and how the Channel Tunnel was dug.

Tunnels by Chris Oxlade (Heinemann, 2005)
Good images and useful information about materials and construction techniques for different tunnels.

Films

The Wooden Horse directed by Jack Lee (Warner Home Video, 1950)
This black-and-white film tells the story of the Wooden Horse escape.

The Great Escape directed by John Sturges (MGM, 1963)
This is a classic World War II action movie based on a true story of escape from Stalag Luft III.

Websites

Underground railway systems:
http://photos. ltmcollection.org/
Photographic archive of London Transport, including the construction of the London Underground.

Sutton Hoo:
www.archaeology.co.uk/ ca/timeline/saxon/sutton hoo/suttonhoo.htm
The story of the excavation of Sutton Hoo, the findings and their history.

The Channel Tunnel:
www.theotherside.co.uk/ tm-heritage/background/ tunnel.htm#info
The history of the construction of the Channel Tunnel.

www.urbanrail.net/
Descriptions of the world's metro systems.

Index

Anning, Mary 28
archaeologists 22, 23

Berlin Wall 8, 9
burials 22, 23, 24, 25, 26
Butterworth, Peter 7

Carter, Howard 20, 21
catacombs 24, 25
cavers 10
Channel Tunnel 14, 15
coffins 26, 27

de Gamond, Thomé 14
dinosaurs 28, 29

Egypt 20
Elandsrand mine 12
engineers 14, 16, 17
Eurostar 14

fossils 28, 29

gold mines 12, 13

Hiroshima 18
Houdini, Harry 27

Krubera Cave 10

landmines 8, 9
Lewis, Owain 29
London 16, 18

miners 12, 13
morgue 24
Mount Weather, USA 19
mummy 20

Nazis 4, 6
New York underground 16
nuclear bombs 18

Paris 16, 17, 24
prison camps 4, 6
pterosaur 29

Saxon king 22
ship burial 22, 23
speleology 10
stalactites 11
Stalag Luft III 4, 6
stalagmites 11
Sutton Hoo ship burial
    22, 23
swimming pool 27

Tokyo underground 16
tombs 20, 21
train tunnel 14
Tutankhamun 20, 21

underground railways
    16, 17

World War II 4